W9-BVR-378

Popular Rock Superstars of Yesterday and Today
POP ROCK

AC/DC

Aerosmith

The Allman
Brothers Band

The Beatles

Billy Joel

Bob Marley
and the Wailers

Bruce Springsteen

The Doors

Elton John

The Grateful Dead

Led Zeppelin

Lynyrd Skynyrd

Pink Floyd

Queen

The Rolling
Stones

U2

The Who

The Beatles

Jim Gallagher

Mason Crest Publishers

The Beatles

FRONTIS Perhaps more than any musician before them, John, Paul, Ringo, and George——the Beatles——changed the face of music.

Author acknowledgment: For Randy Pile, who first turned me on to the Beatles.

Produced by 21st Century Publishing and Communications, Inc.

Editorial by Harding House Publishing Services, Inc.

MASON CREST PUBLISHERS INC.
370 Reed Road
Broomall, Pennsylvania 19008
(866) MCP-BOOK (toll free)
www.masoncrest.com

Printed in the United States.

Second Printing

9 8 7 6 5 4 3 2

Library of Congress Cataloging-in-Publication Data

Gallagher, Jim, 1969–
  The Beatles / Jim Gallagher.
    p. cm. — (Popular rock superstars of yesterday and today)
  Includes bibliographical references (p.   ) and index.
  Hardback edition: ISBN-13: 978-1-4222-0186-2
  Paperback edition: ISBN-13: 978-1-4222-0311-8
 1. Beatles—Juvenile literature. 2. Rock musicians—England—Biography—
Juvenile literature. I. Title.
ML3930.B39G38 2008
782.42166092'2—dc22
[B]   2007012149

CONTENTS

Rock 'n' Roll Timeline

1951
"Rocket 88," considered by many to be the first rock single, is released by Ike Turner.

1952
DJ Alan Freed coins and popularizes the term "Rock and Roll," proclaimes himself the "Father of Rock and Roll," and declares, "Rock and Roll is a river of music that has absorbed many streams: rhythm and blues, jazz, rag time, cowboy songs, country songs, folk songs. All have contributed to the Big Beat."

1955
"Rock Around the Clock" by Bill Haley & His Comets is released; it tops the U.S. charts and becomes wildly popular in Britain, Australia, and Germany.

1969
The Woodstock Music and Arts Festival attracts a huge crowd to rural upstate New York.

1969
Tommy, the first rock opera, is released by British rock band The Who.

1970
The Beatles break up.

1967
The Monterey Pop Festival in California kicks off open air rock concerts.

1965
The psychedelic rock band, the Grateful Dead, is formed in San Francisco.

1971
Jim Morrison, lead singer of The Doors, dies in Paris.

1971
Duane Allman, lead guitarist of the Allman Brothers Band, dies.

1950s   1960s   1970s

1957
Bill Haley tours Europe.

1957
Jerry Lee Lewis and Buddy Holly become the first rock musicians to tour Australia.

1954
Elvis Presley releases the extremely popular single "That's All Right (Mama)."

1961
The first Grammy for Best Rock 'n' Roll Recording is awarded to Chubby Checker for *Let's Twist Again*.

1964
The Beatles make their first visit to America, setting off the British Invasion.

1969
A rock concert held at Altamont Speedway in California is marred by violence.

1969
The Rolling Stones tour America as "The Greatest Rock and Roll Band in the World."

1973
Rolling Stone magazine names Annie Leibovitz chief photographer and "rock 'n' roll photographer;" she follows and photographs rockers Mick Jagger, John Lennon, and others.

1974
Sheer Heart Attack by the British rock band Queen becomes an international success.

1974
"Sweet Home Alabama" by Southern rock band Lynyrd Skynyrd is released and becomes an American anthem.

1987
Billy Joel becomes the first American rock star to perform in the Soviet Union since the construction of the Berlin Wall.

2005
Led Zeppelin is ranked #1 on VH1's list of the 100 Greatest Artists of Hard Rock.

2005
Many rock groups participate in Live 8, a series of concerts to raise awareness of extreme poverty in Africa.

1985
Rock stars perform at Live Aid, a benefit concert to raise money to fight Ethiopian famine.

2003
Led Zeppelin's "Stairway to Heaven" is inducted into the Grammy Hall of Fame.

1980
John Lennon of the Beatles is murdered in New York City.

2000s
Aerosmith's album sales reach 140 million worldwide and the group becomes the bestselling American hard rock band of all time.

2007
Billy Joel become the first person to sing the National Anthem before two Super Bowls.

1975
Tommy, the movie, is released.

1975
Time magazine features Bruce Springsteen on its cover as "Rock's New Sensation."

1995
The Rock and Roll Hall of Fame and Museum opens in Cleveland, Ohio.

1970s   1980s   1990s   2000s

1979
Pink Floyd's *The Wall* is released.

1991
Freddie Mercury, lead vocalist of the British rock group Queen, dies of AIDS.

2004
Elton John receives a Kennedy Center Honor.

1979
The first Grammy for Best Rock Vocal Performance by a Duo or Group is awarded to The Eagles.

2004
Rolling Stone Magazine ranks The Beatles #1 of the 100 Greatest Artists of All Time, and Bob Dylan #2.

1986
The Rolling Stones receive a Grammy Lifetime Achievement Award.

1981
MTV goes on the air.

2006
U2 wins five more Grammys, for a total of 22—the most of any rock artist or group.

1986
The first Rock and Roll Hall of Fame induction ceremony is held; Chuck Berry, Little Richard, Ray Charles, Elvis Presley, and James Brown, are among the first inductees.

1981
For Those About to Rock We Salute You by Australian rock band AC/DC becomes the first hard rock album to reach #1 in the U.S.

2006
Bob Dylan, at age 65, releases *Modern Times* which immediately rises to #1 in the U.S.

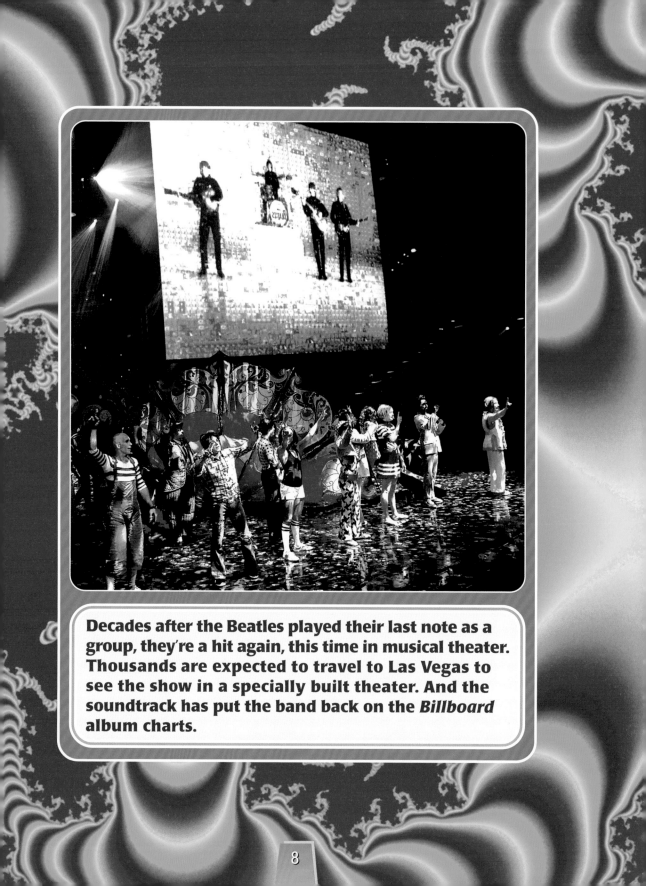

Decades after the Beatles played their last note as a group, they're a hit again, this time in musical theater. Thousands are expected to travel to Las Vegas to see the show in a specially built theater. And the soundtrack has put the band back on the *Billboard* album charts.

1

Love

More than forty years after their first hit, the Beatles continue to exert a great influence on popular music and culture. People all over the world still enjoy the music created by band members John Lennon, Paul McCartney, George Harrison, and Ringo Starr. In 2006, the Beatles' history and musical legacy was explored in a new musical titled *Love*.

For the Las Vegas show, the Beatles' company, Apple Corps, collaborated with the world-renowned entertainment company Cirque du Soleil. In *Love*, Cirque du Soleil acrobats and dancers are accompanied by Beatles music as they attempt to tell stories through their movements and gestures. According to a promotional Web site for the show,

"*Love* brings the magic of Cirque du Soleil together with the spirit and passion behind the most beloved rock group of all time to create a vivid, intimate and powerful entertainment experience. *Love* evokes the exuberant

and irreverent spirit of the Beatles, as interpreted through the youthful, urban energy of a cast of 60 international artists.

A special theater, which includes a unique sound system, was constructed for the show at the Mirage casino in Las Vegas, at a cost of more than $100 million. *Love* is expected to run at the Mirage for several years.

All You Need Is *Love*

The idea for *Love* came out of conversations between George Harrison and Cirque du Soleil co-founder Guy Laliberté in 2000. After George's death in 2001, his widow Olivia and his friend Neil Aspinall, the director of Apple Corps, kept the idea alive. Eventually, the other surviving Beatles agreed to allow the show to be created.

To create music for the show, Cirque du Soleil turned to producer George Martin, who had worked on most of the Beatles' albums. Martin, who has sometimes been called the "fifth Beatle" because of his contributions in the recording studio, asked his son Giles to help with the project. Together, they sorted through hours of original tapes recorded by the band between 1963 and 1970. They created a **mash-up** by taking a number of the band's best-known hits and adding bits of music or lyrics from some Beatles songs that are less well known.

The project took more than two years, but the band members were very pleased with the outcome. Ringo later commented,

George and Giles did such a great job combining these tracks. It's really powerful for me and I even heard things I'd forgotten we'd recorded.

After months of rehearsals and a series of preview performances, *Love* officially opened on June 30, 2006. Among those who attended were former Beatles Paul McCartney and Ringo Starr, as well as John Lennon's widow Yoko Ono; John's former wife Cynthia and their son Julian; George's widow Olivia and their son Dhani; and George Martin.

New Album Released

In November 2006, the **soundtrack** to the show was released. It was an immediate success all over the world, selling more than 5 million copies in its first six weeks on the market. In the United States, the album sold more than a million copies and reached the #4 spot on the *Billboard* album chart.

Most music critics liked the remixes, and nearly all reviews of the new album were positive. In the *Orlando Sentinel*, reviewer Jim Abbott wrote:

THE BEATLES™

LOVE™

CIRQUE DU SOLEIL®

AT THE MIRAGE

Love **is a collaboration between Apple Corps and the legendary Cirque du Soleil. Music and a cast of sixty international performers combine to bring to the audience scenes inspired by the Beatles' memorable lyrics. The show features such diverse theatrics as aerial performances, dance, and even extreme sports. It's an experience audience members aren't likely to forget.**

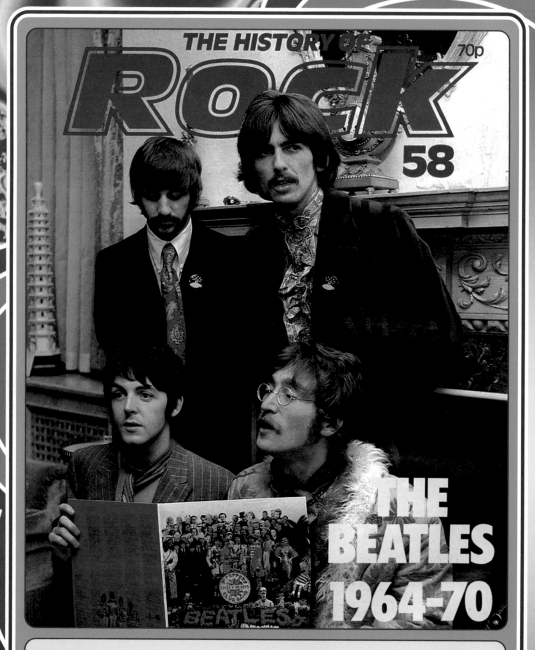

THE HISTORY OF ROCK

70p

58

THE BEATLES 1964-70

Some critics have called the Beatles the most influential rock group of all time. Their importance in the history of rock music is without question, as evidenced by the group's appearance on the cover of volume 58 of *The History of Rock*. In a genre that seems to create many one-hit wonders, the Beatles had fifty-two top-40 hits.

"*[Love]* mixes familiar classics in unexpected ways that ultimately enliven the music by allowing listeners to experience it from new angles. . . . Many would argue that it's impossible to improve on the originals, but *Love* succeeds at its equally **audacious** mission: It updates this timeless music without dishonoring it."

Timeless Music

Growing up during the 1940s and 1950s in Liverpool, a war-ravaged industrial city in northern England, John, Paul, George, and Ringo could never have imagined the impact their music would have. But today, many rock groups—from U2 and Bruce Springsteen to Nirvana and Oasis—credit the Beatles as their inspiration. The Beatles are generally considered the greatest and most influential rock group of all time.

Although the band's recording career lasted less than a decade, from their first hit in 1963 to their breakup in 1970, the Beatles produced more than 400 songs. They had twenty #1 singles, more than any other artist (Elvis Presley is second with seventeen), and their fifty-two top-40 hits are behind only Elvis (104) and Elton John (fifty-nine), both of whom had significantly longer careers. The *Guinness Book of World Records* reports that the Beatles have sold more than a billion records, more than any other rock group in history.

But the Beatles did much more than just sell records. They were a cultural phenomenon during the turbulent 1960s, influencing how people dressed, behaved, and thought. They became famous throughout the world, and their ideas about social issues such as spirituality and the peace movement were taken seriously by people of all ages.

The band also changed the sound of popular music. The Beatles were **innovators** in the recording studio, trying new instruments and techniques to create unusual and interesting effects on their songs. The Beatles also changed the way that music was made. Before their success, many bands played compositions written by professional songwriters. The Beatles wrote their own songs and inspired other musicians to take more control over their music and lyrics.

John, Paul, George, and Ringo had never expected to achieve such fame. The four young men just wanted to make rock 'n' roll music— they had no idea they would make rock 'n' roll history.

They were four young, clean-cut boys from Liverpool, England. Their hair might have been longer than most of the day, but they dressed nicely, and their music was phenomenal. Before long, their music—and their look—would take over rock music in the United States as well as in their native Britain.

2

Origin of the Beatles

The four Beatles were born in Liverpool, England, during World War II (John and Ringo in 1940, Paul in 1942, and George in 1943). Like many teenagers during the 1950s, all four loved rock 'n' roll performers like Chuck Berry, Little Richard, Eddie Cochran, Elvis Presley, and Buddy Holly. Those early rockers inspired the Beatles to become musicians.

A Band Is Formed

In 1957, John Lennon and some of his friends formed a **skiffle** group. Skiffle was a style of music that was very popular in England that year. Skiffle musicians used guitars and homemade instruments to make music. John's band was called the Quarry Men, and they played at many community events.

John met Paul McCartney in July 1957, at a church festival where the Quarry Men had played. At the time they met, Paul was a much better musician. He knew how to play trumpet and piano in addition to guitar. Paul told John that he was playing his guitar chords incorrectly; John had been using the fingering for banjo chords. John later said,

> **Paul taught me how to play properly—but I had to learn the chords left-handed, because Paul is left-handed. So I learnt them upside down, and then I'd go home and reverse them.**

A few months later, Paul introduced John to another guitar player, whom he had met while riding the bus to school. The quiet young man was George Harrison. John was initially skeptical because George was somewhat younger than the others in the group. However, John was impressed when he heard George play guitar because of his talent for picking out solos. George was invited to join the Quarry Men in March 1958 as the lead guitar player.

Becoming the Beatles

Gradually, the Quarry Men became more polished performers. John, Paul, and George formed the core of the band. All three played guitar, with John's friend Stuart Sutcliffe playing bass. Other musicians came and went, and the Quarry Men often played without a drummer.

In May 1960, the Quarry Men were offered a job as the backup band for a singer named Johnny Gentle, who was going to perform a series of shows in Scotland. Although they made little money, the band gained valuable stage experience. George later remembered:

> **That was our first professional gig: on a tour of dance halls miles up in the North of Scotland. We felt, 'Yippee, we've got a gig!' Then we realized that we were playing to nobody in little halls. . . . The band was horrible, an embarrassment. We didn't have amplifiers or anything.**

During the tour, an experienced drummer named Tommy Moore had accompanied the Quarry Men. Afterward, the band members decided they needed a full-time drummer. Tommy wasn't interested, so Paul played drums for a while. However, he preferred guitar, so in August 1960 drummer Pete Best was invited to join the band.

Around the same time, the group changed its name to the Beatles. The band members liked this new name because it included a "beat," just like their music. It was also similar to the name of Buddy Holly's

The original Beatles—the Quarry Men—were Ringo-less. For a while, there was no permanent drummer, with even Paul occasionally acting as stick man. When the group decided to become the Beatles, they also made the decision to hire a permanent drummer: Pete Best, seen in this photo. He didn't turn out to be very permanent, though.

band, the Crickets. In 1961 John wrote a humorous essay in which he revealed the inspiration for the name:

> **It came in a vision—a man appeared on a flaming pie and said unto them, 'From this day on you are Beatles with an A.'—'Thank you, Mister Man,' they said, thanking him.**

The Beatles soon became one of the best-known bands in Liverpool. They attracted large crowds to the nightclubs where they played. Because of their popularity, in late 1960 the Beatles were invited to spend a month playing nightclubs in Hamburg, Germany. In Hamburg, the band played six nights a week, sometimes performing for eight hours or more. The Beatles learned a great deal about how to please an audience. As John later said,

> **We got better and got more confidence. We couldn't help it, with all the experience, playing all night long.**

Under New Management

The Beatles returned to Hamburg in 1961. During this trip, Stuart Sutcliffe decided to quit the band and stay in Hamburg with his German girlfriend. Paul agreed to become the bass player. Because he was left-handed, he had to learn how to play the instrument upside down.

When the Beatles returned to Liverpool, they were offered a job with singer Tony Sheridan, who had just received a recording contract. In June 1961, the band went into a professional recording studio for the first time. They recorded music for Sheridan's album, including a rock 'n' roll version of the song "My Bonnie."

One day someone walked into the North End Music Store in Liverpool and asked the owner, Brian Epstein, for the recording of "My Bonnie." Epstein had never heard of the record, but promised to find it for his customer. When Epstein heard the record, he became interested in the Beatles. He went to watch the band play at the Cavern Club in Liverpool. Impressed, he offered to manage the band and help the Beatles get a recording contract.

He started as the owner of a Liverpool music store, but Brian Epstein (second from right in this early photo) would move into a position to play a significant role in Beatle history. When he became the group's manager, their hair changed, and their onstage behavior changed as well when they began to bow at performance end.

When the Beatles agreed to this deal, Brian told them they needed to make some changes in order to be successful. The Beatles cut their hair differently, began wearing nicer outfits on stage, and started bowing together at the end of shows. Brian also paid for the band to go back into the recording studio and produce a **demo tape**. Then he mailed copies of the tape to executives in the music business. But although the band had several auditions, no one was interested in signing them to a contract.

Meeting George Martin

In July 1962, a young producer at EMI Records named George Martin agreed to work with the Beatles. He would record several of their songs and release them as singles. If one of them became a hit, EMI would record and release an album of the band's music.

Martin did not think Pete Best was a very good drummer, so he insisted that the band replace him. There had been other problems with Pete, so John, Paul, and George agreed. To take his place, the

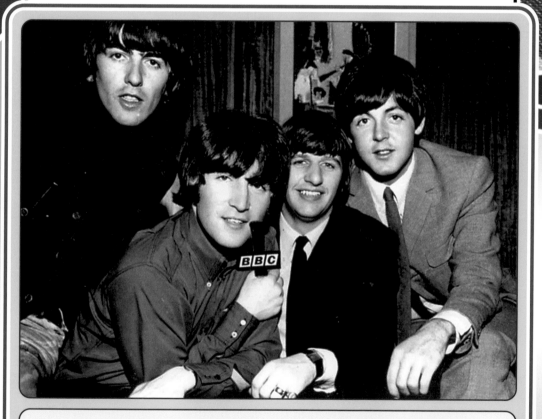

Once the Beatles met record producer George Martin— sometimes called the fifth Beatle—more things changed. He told the band to change drummers, so Richard Starkey— Ringo—joined the group. George, John, Ringo, and Paul are shown in this photo from a BBC radio program. The Beatles were frequent guests on BBC Radio, especially as their popularity soared.

Beatles asked a drummer named Ringo Starr, whom they had gotten to know in Hamburg, to join the band.

In September 1962, the Beatles went into the EMI studios and recorded several songs that John and Paul had written. Their first song to be released as a single, "Love Me Do," reached #17 on the British pop charts. The second song, "Please Please Me," did even better, becoming the Beatles' first #1 hit.

Excited by this success, George Martin quickly brought the band back into the studios to make their first album. *Please Please Me* was recorded in twelve hours, and soon hit the top of the British charts. In 1963, the Beatles recorded and released two more #1 singles, "From Me to You" and "She Loves You."

Because of their growing popularity, the Beatles were invited to perform several short concerts aired throughout 1963 by the British Broadcasting Corporation (BBC). For the band members, one of the highlights of the year was playing live on the country's most popular television show, *Sunday Night at the London Palladium*, in October. By the end of 1963, the Beatles had established themselves as the hottest group in Britain. Now they were ready for a new challenge: conquering America.

When the Beatles arrived in the United States in 1964 (seen in this photo), it was like nothing ever before seen in the country. Huge crowds of screaming fans greeted the four "mop-tops" from Britain at every stop on the Beatles' tour. It's easy to see how American rock bands might have felt neglected!

3

Beatlemania

On February 9, 1964, approximately 73 million Americans watched John, Paul, George, and Ringo perform five songs on the *Ed Sullivan Show*. Their electrifying performance ensured that the Beatles would become stars in the United States. The term "Beatlemania" was soon coined to describe the group's enthusiastic fans, who screamed every time a band member opened his mouth to sing.

Americans had already heard of the Beatles before they appeared on the *Ed Sullivan Show*. In January, their single "I Want to Hold Your Hand" sold a million copies in less than ten days, setting a music industry record. And approximately 3,000 screaming fans were waiting at New York's Kennedy Airport when the Beatles arrived for their first visit to the United States. But Beatlemania grew more intense after the television show, and huge crowds came to see the band in Washington, D.C., Miami, and other American cities.

It soon became impossible for the Beatles to go out in public without guards. Everywhere they went, crowds of people mobbed them, trying to touch them or asking for their autographs. One night, someone even cut off a handful of Ringo's hair. The Beatles did not like this aspect of their fame, but they tried to keep a sense of humor about Beatlemania. Paul later commented:

> **"The thing is, we never really believed in Beatlemania, never took the whole thing seriously, I suppose. That way, we managed to stay sane."**

By April 1964, it was obvious that the Beatles had won over American audiences in the same way they had conquered Britain and other countries. That month five of their songs—"Can't Buy Me Love," "Twist and Shout," "She Loves You," "I Want to Hold Your Hand," and "Please Please Me"—held the top five spots on the *Billboard* chart. That was a feat no other rock performer had ever accomplished.

The success of the Beatles in the mid-1960s helped to launch the so-called "British Invasion," opening the U.S. market for other British groups like the Rolling Stones, the Kinks, the Who, and the Animals.

A Hard Year's Work

To capitalize on their fame, the Beatles agreed to star in a movie that would feature some of their songs. Richard Lester, who had made a film that all four Beatles admired, was hired to direct. They decided to call the movie *A Hard Day's Night*. Writer Alun Owen spent a few days with the band, and then wrote a script based on his observations. Ringo later commented,

> **"[Owen] came on part of our British tour and wrote down the chaos that went on around us, and how we lived, and gave us a caricature of ourselves. So *A Hard Day's Night* was like a day in the life; or really, two days and two nights of our life."**

The movie, which featured many new songs by John and Paul, was a major international hit. The new music included on the album *A Hard Day's Night* sold very well.

It wasn't just teenage girls who got caught up in Beatlemania. Other celebrities wanted to be associated with the group. In this 1964 photo, Muhammad Ali (then known as Cassius Clay) stands triumphant after "knocking out" John, Paul, Ringo, and George, who seem to be pleading for their lives on the ring floor.

Although the band members spent most of their time working, they also found time for personal relationships. George began dating Pattie Boyd, a model he had met while filming *A Hard Day's Night*, while Paul started dating model Jane Asher. Ringo was still with

George, Ringo, Paul, and John are getting their hairstyle touched up in this photo from the set of the group's first film, *A Hard Day's Night*. The world couldn't get enough of the Beatles, so management hopped on the opportunity to put the guys in a movie. Like almost everything the group touched, the film was a huge hit.

Maureen Cox, his girlfriend from before the Beatles' days. John was settling into a new home with his wife Cynthia and their son Julian, who had been born in 1963. (Brian had insisted that John's 1962 marriage to Cynthia be kept a secret, because he was afraid female fans would lose interest in the band if they knew John was married.)

After a short vacation, the band went on a world tour, performing in Scandinavia, Holland, Hong Kong, Australia, and New Zealand. In every city they visited, large crowds turned out to see them. The Beatles then returned to America for a five-week tour, playing for crowds in larger **venues**. In October, they toured Britain.

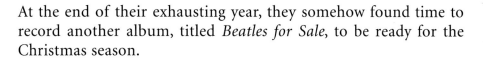

At the end of their exhausting year, they somehow found time to record another album, titled *Beatles for Sale*, to be ready for the Christmas season.

Growing as Artists

The Beatles continued working hard in 1965. Because of the success of *A Hard Day's Night*, they agreed to make another movie with Richard Lester. This time, the film would have a much different plot. *Help!* was about a special ring that Ringo found. All through the film, people were trying to catch Ringo to get the ring, while the other Beatles tried to protect him.

Once again, Paul and John wrote most of the songs, although George contributed two songs to the soundtrack. John contributed the title track, "Help!," which became a #1 hit. John later explained that "Help!" reflected the pressure he felt about the Beatles' success. At the same time, Paul wrote the song "Yesterday," which became another major hit for the band.

Overall, music critics agreed that the Beatles' lyrics were becoming deeper and more interesting. Paul later explained that

"Things were changing. The direction was moving away from the poppy stuff like 'Thank You Girl,' 'From Me to You,' and 'She Loves You.' . . . Now we'd come to a point where we thought, 'We've done that. Now we can branch out into songs that are more surreal, a little more entertaining.'"

John and Paul credited songwriters like Bob Dylan, whom they had met during their 1964 American tour, for inspiring their more meaningful lyrics. Dylan had another important influence on the band as well—he introduced them to marijuana. Later, the members of the Beatles would try other drugs, such as LSD (lysergic acid diethylamide). They believed these drugs helped them to hear and see things differently, and to be more creative.

In July 1965, the Beatles learned that the British government wanted to give them medals as a reward for their accomplishments. This was a great honor. Some people argued that the Beatles did not deserve the award, and a few war veterans even returned their medals in protest. The band members eventually received their medals from Queen Elizabeth II at a special ceremony.

Back on the Road

In the summer of 1965, the Beatles went back on tour. They performed in France, Italy, and Spain before returning to the United States, where they were booked in large sports stadiums. Their first stadium show, held at New York's Shea Stadium in August, drew 55,000 fans. It was the biggest rock concert ever held up until that time.

For the Beatles, a highlight of the tour was meeting Elvis Presley. The "king of rock 'n' roll" was in Los Angeles making a movie, and John, Paul, George, and Ringo spent an evening jamming with him at his rented home.

When the tour ended, the Beatles went back into the studio to record their next album. Even more than *Help!*, this record would show how the group's songwriting was maturing. But the song lyrics weren't the only new things. George played an Indian instrument called a sitar on the song "Norwegian Wood," and new sounds and tape effects were incorporated into the music. The result was *Rubber Soul*, an innovative album that was widely praised by music critics. George later said,

> **"*Rubber Soul* was my favorite album, even at that time. I think that it was the best one we made; we certainly knew we were making a good album. We did spend a bit more time on it and tried new things. . . . Also, we were being more influenced by other people's music and everything was blossoming at that time, including us, because we were still growing."**

Studio Innovation

By the beginning of 1966, the four Beatles decided they needed a break. They had been performing and traveling together almost constantly since the early 1960s. For a few months, they relaxed in London. On January 21, George married Pattie Boyd, with Paul serving as best man.

John, Paul, Ringo, and George hit the road again in 1965, playing before huge crowds in Europe and a record-breaking performance at New York's Shea Stadium in the United States. The group's success was even too much for the Queen of England to ignore, and the group members received medals in recognition of their accomplishments.

By April, the band was ready to get back to the studio and expand on the musical ideas of *Rubber Soul*. George had become very interested in Indian music, so he brought his sitar along with several other instruments. New equipment allowed voices to be **double-tracked**, producing a different sound. The band also experimented with adding random sounds to some songs. They recorded sounds, like someone hitting a glass with a pencil, then played the tapes back while they recorded their songs. Sometimes they played tapes backward,

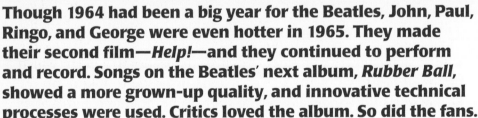

Though 1964 had been a big year for the Beatles, John, Paul, Ringo, and George were even hotter in 1965. They made their second film—*Help!*—and they continued to perform and record. Songs on the Beatles' next album, *Rubber Ball*, showed a more grown-up quality, and innovative technical processes were used. Critics loved the album. So did the fans.

which created an even more unusual sound. All these tricks would be incorporated into the *Revolver* album.

Usually, musical groups would go on tour to promote their new songs. However, new singles like "Rain," where the guitar and drum parts had been taped and played backward on the final recording, could not be played properly in front of an audience. The Beatles had to come up with another way to promote their new songs. According to George:

> **"The technology we were now using on records didn't allow us to play a lot of songs live on tour. In those days there was no technology on stage, as there is now. There were two guitars, bass and drums, and that was it. If we did stuff in the studio with the aid of recording tricks, then we couldn't reproduce them on tour."**

The band's solution was to make short films to promote the singles "Paperback Writer" and "Rain." These films, which would be shown on television, were the forerunners of modern music videos.

The Beatles were tired of touring anyway. In five years they had played more than 1,400 concerts all over the world, and they wanted to spend more time working on their music in the recording studio. And their touring experiences in the summer of 1966 would make it easy for them to give up life on the road.

Troubled Times on Tour

In the summer of 1966, the Beatles began a world tour. The first two countries were fine. First they visited Germany and were happy to see some old friends from their Hamburg days. Then it was on to Tokyo, where they played several concerts. When the group reached the Philippines, however, the band ran into problems. Imelda Marcos, the wife of that country's president, invited the Beatles to a party, which the band politely declined. Marcos was not used to taking no for an answer, and she became very angry. The next day, newspaper headlines reported, "Beatles Snub First Lady."

Angered at this insult, the people of the Philippines turned against the band. The hotel staff refused to serve them food or take care of their things. When they traveled, crowds shouted at them. Even the local police, who were supposed to protect the band, tried to intimidate them. The Beatles were afraid they might be arrested or attacked, so they decided to leave. However, their plane was held on the runway

涙の乗車券

チケット・トゥ・ライド
TICKET TO RIDE

イエス・イット・イズ
YES IT IS

ビートルズ

Odeon RECORDS

芝音楽工業株式会社 FY 330

The world beckoned the Beatles again in 1966, and they answered with another tour. A reunion tour of Germany was followed by a trip to Japan. The Beatles were very popular in Japan, even though many in the crowd might not have known what the group's lyrics meant. The next stop on the tour—the Philippines—was not so successful.

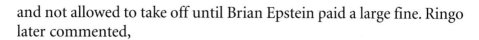

and not allowed to take off until Brian Epstein paid a large fine. Ringo later commented,

> **"The Philippines visit was very frightening. It's probably the most frightening thing that's happened to me."**

On the way home, the Beatles decided to visit India for a short vacation. The country fascinated all four band members. George was particularly interested, as he had already begun reading about **yoga** and Indian philosophy and listening to traditional Indian music.

More Problems

When the Beatles returned home to prepare for their upcoming U.S. tour, they had to deal with a new problem. Back in March, the band had done a newspaper interview in which John had made a comment about the band's fame, saying "We're more popular than Jesus now." For months no one had noticed, but in July, an American magazine had publicized the quote. Taken out of the context of the original article, the comment angered many Christians, particularly in the Southern states. Conservatives began protesting against the band and destroying their albums.

Even though John apologized, the American tour did not go well. John later said,

> **"I can't imagine any reason which would make us do any sort of tour again. We're all really tired. It does nothing for us any more. . . . The music wasn't being heard. It was just a sort of a freak show. The Beatles *were* the show, and the music had nothing to do with it."**

When the band played in Shea Stadium, 11,000 seats went unsold. The Beatles received death threats, and crowds of angry people protested when they played shows in the South. The band played its final show at Candlestick Park in San Francisco.

Things changed for the group in the late 1960s, including their look. Following the disastrous Philippine tour in 1966, the group decided to take some down time. After all, the Beatles had been performing, recording, and touring almost nonstop. In this photo, longer-haired John, Ringo, Paul, and George (left to right) are shown relaxing.

4

Hello Good-Bye

The public criticism of the Beatles and their decision to stop touring did not affect the response to *Revolver*, which was released in August 1966. The album reached #1 in both the United States and Great Britain. Even today, *Revolver* is considered one of the best rock albums of all time.

The Beatles took some time off during the fall of 1966. John and Paul were particularly interested in **avant-garde** art, and both visited galleries to learn about new trends and fashions. At one exhibit, John met a Japanese artist named Yoko Ono. John was unhappy in his marriage, and he would eventually start an affair with Yoko.

Around this time the Beatles' look began to change. The band members began to appear with longer hair, mustaches, and colorful clothes. The Beatles were always trendsetters, and their new appearance influenced many people.

Sgt. Pepper

The Beatles went back into the studio in November 1966 to record material for a new album. Paul came up with an interesting concept for the record. He later explained:

> **"I took an idea back to the guys in London: 'As we're trying to get away from ourselves—to get away from touring and into a more surreal thing—how about if we become an alter-ego band, something like, say, "Sgt Pepper's Lonely Hearts"? I've got a little bit of a song cooking with that title.'"**

The Beatles spent months in the studio, once again trying to push the limits of the recording equipment. When the album *Sgt. Pepper's Lonely Hearts Club Band* was released in June 1967, it was clear that the band had succeeded. The album was praised for its creative music, poetic song lyrics, and **psychedelic** imagery. Even the cover was unusual. It featured the band members in brightly colored uniforms, standing in front of a collage of influential people.

Sgt. Pepper's Lonely Hearts Club Band was the first rock album to win a Grammy Award. Some forty years after its release, the album still sounds fresh and interesting. In 2003, *Rolling Stone* magazine rated *Sgt. Pepper's* the greatest rock album of all time.

Seeking Guidance

In late August, George invited Paul and John to see a lecture by Maharishi Mahesh Yogi, an Indian **guru**, in London. Maharishi claimed that he had developed a way for people to find inner peace through meditation. The band members were impressed with Maharishi's lecture. Afterward, he invited them to visit him in Bangor, Wales, to learn how to meditate.

While the Beatles were in Wales with Maharishi, they received upsetting news. Their manager, Brian Epstein, had died of a drug overdose. The Beatles were devastated. Brian was a friend—he was not much older than they were—and had played a large role in their success. The Beatles all spoke about how much Brian had meant to them, with Ringo commenting,

The Beatles' 1967 album *Sgt. Pepper's Lonely Hearts Club Band* was very different from anything the group had done before. Lyrics were more creative, more poetic. And the cover was, well, unusual—at least for the Beatles. Critics and the fans all loved the album. So did the Grammy Awards.

"We loved Brian. He was a generous man. We owe so much to him. We have come a long way with Brian along the same road."

Brian was someone the four Beatles trusted. In addition to taking care of their business arrangements, he had resolved disagreements among the band members fairly. Without him to defuse tensions, the relationship between John, Paul, George, and Ringo grew strained.

Business Troubles

The Beatles' first project without Brian was a disaster. Paul had suggested making an unscripted film featuring the band riding through England on a bus with other passengers. *The Magical Mystery Tour* was shown on British television in late December 1967. Although there were some funny parts, many people did not like the movie. The response was so bad that the Beatles decided not to release the film in the United States.

The soundtrack to the film fared much better. It was nominated for a Grammy Award and included such hits as "The Fool on the Hill" and "I Am the Walrus."

In January 1968, the Beatles formed Apple Corps, a company to oversee their affairs. At a press conference, Paul and John explained that in addition to promoting the Beatles, the company would help other creative musicians and artists start their careers. In addition to a record label, Apple included a film production company, an electronics division responsible for creating new gadgets, and even a clothing store called the Apple Boutique.

However, the Beatles proved to be poor businessmen. The film and electronics divisions lost a lot of money, and the clothing store had to be closed after only six months. The Beatles ended up giving most of the clothes away. The only profitable division was Apple Records.

A Visit to India

In early 1968, the four Beatles took a trip to India to spend more time studying with the Maharishi. Other celebrities were there as well, including the British pop singer Donovan, Mike Love of the Beach Boys, and the American actress Mia Farrow. The Beatles later admitted that they were looking for the meaning of life. Paul explained:

> **"I think by 1968 we were all a bit exhausted, spiritually. We'd been the Beatles, which was marvelous. . . . but I think generally there was a feeling of: 'Yeah, well, it's great to be famous, it's great to be rich—but what's it all for?'"**

The Beatles eventually decided that meditation was not the answer either. All four left India disillusioned with the Maharishi and his

In the fall of 1967, George, Paul, and John first met the Indian guru Maharishi Mahesh Yogi. The pressure of being the top in their field weighed heavy on the guys, and they sought to gain a deeper understanding of the spiritual. In this photo, Paul, George, and Ringo meet with the Maharishi during a 1968 visit to India.

methods. But their time in the mountains had been well spent. The four Beatles returned with many new songs for their next album.

Yoko and the White Album

In May 1968, John and Cynthia Lennon's marriage finally broke up. John wanted a divorce because he had started an intense love affair with Yoko Ono. John was so in love with Yoko that he refused to let her leave his side, even when the Beatles went back into the recording studio. However, her presence in the studio annoyed the other Beatles, who felt she was distracting John from their music. According to George Martin:

"There was a huge bond between John and Yoko. There's no doubt about it: they were completely together mentally and I think that as that bond grew, so John lessened his bond with Paul and the others—which obviously caused problems."

Did she or didn't she break up the Beatles? Many point to John's relationship with the artist Yoko Ono as the beginning of the end for the group. Whether or not the John-and-Yoko relationship was responsible for the breakup, there was no question that the pair had an intensely close bond. They seemed to be true soul mates.

Yoko's presence was not the only reason recording sessions were tense. In the past, all four Beatles had contributed to the writing of new songs. Now, Paul, John, and George each had strong ideas about how their songs should sound, and none of them were as open to suggestions from the others. Things became so uncomfortable that Ringo even quit the band for about two weeks. However, he returned to finish the album without the public finding out.

Despite the tension, the **double album** was another great success when it was released in November 1968. Officially titled *The Beatles*, the record is unofficially known as the "White Album" because of the record's plain white cover. The songs on the album are quite varied—from pop songs like "Back in the U.S.S.R." to the heavier-sounding "Helter Skelter," and from traditional ballads like "Blackbird" and "Julia" to the avant-garde "Revolution 9," an unusual track created by John and Yoko.

Continuing Problems

In January 1969, the Beatles started a new project, which they called "Get Back." The idea was to make a movie of the band working on new songs and then playing them in a concert. The four Beatles would jam together as they had in the early days, and the album would have the raw, exciting feel of live music.

Unfortunately, none of the Beatles enjoyed the project. To get the songs right without editing them in the studio, they had to record each one dozens of times. This was very tedious. Also, having every moment filmed felt awkward, especially because of the band's inner tensions. Yoko was in the studio every day, and the other Beatles began to feel that Paul was trying to boss them around. Things got so bad that George walked out after a fight with Paul.

When George came back, he brought a talented keyboard player named Billy Preston with him. Billy had an easygoing personality, and his presence helped ease the friction in the studio. The band enjoyed having him around, and he played on several songs.

For the concert to end the movie, the band decided to perform on the roof of their office building. On January 30, 1969, the Beatles and Billy Preston played several songs before the police arrived and told them to stop. No one knew it at the time, but this would be the band's last public show.

A new film was in the works for the band in 1969, but this one would be different. This film would be about process—the way new songs are developed. The plan was for it to be like the old days, full of mutual creativity and jamming, and to end with a concert on the roof of their office building.

Work on the documentary film moved forward, but the band was not sure what to do with the songs they had recorded. George Martin tried to make them into an album, but no one was happy with it. The Beatles decided to put the recording aside for a while.

You Never Give Me Your Money

With Apple Corps losing money, the Beatles decided to hire a new manager to take charge of their business affairs. However, the band members could not agree on who should represent them. John, George, and Ringo wanted Allen Klein, an American accountant who managed the Rolling Stones. However, Paul did not trust Klein. Instead, he hired Lee Eastman, the father of his new girlfriend Linda, to represent him in business dealings. The arguments over financial matters divided the band members further.

When Klein took control of Apple Corps, he negotiated a new deal with the Beatles' record companies, so that they made more money from each record sold. He also reorganized Apple, firing many employees in order to save money. In addition, he hired an American producer named Phil Spector and told him to make an album from the Get Back recordings. (This record would be retitled *Let It Be.*)

On March 12, 1969, Paul married Linda Eastman in a small ceremony. As a sign of how bad things had gotten, the other Beatles were not invited. Two weeks later, John and Yoko flew to Gibraltar and were married. They used their honeymoon as a platform to talk publicly about their opposition to war. For eight days, they permitted reporters to interview them as they relaxed in a large bed. They called it a "bed-in for peace."

Abbey Road

In April 1969, the Beatles decided to try recording another album. Although the band's problems continued, somehow John, Paul, George, and Ringo put together another excellent album, which they called *Abbey Road*. Ringo later said:

❝After the *Let It Be* nightmare, *Abbey Road* turned out fine. The second side is brilliant. Out of the ashes of all that madness, that last section is for me one of the finest pieces we put together.❞

It was on *Abbey Road* that George emerged as a songwriter equal to John or Paul. His single "Something" was a #1 hit in the United States and has become one of the most popular rock songs of all time. Another of George's tunes, "Here Comes the Sun," was written with his friend Eric Clapton. It described George's feelings of relief when the uncomfortable recording sessions ended each day.

The last section of *Abbey Road* is a long **montage** of songs written by Paul and John. The last part of this medley is titled "The End," and

One of the most famous album covers of all times is the one designed for *Abbey Road*. Much speculation surrounded Paul's appearance on the cover barefoot, out of step, and eyes closed. For years it fueled rumors that Paul was dead. The album was a huge success, and George took his place as a talented songwriter in his own right.

features Paul, George, and then John playing guitar solos, followed by the only drum solo Ringo ever recorded on a Beatles album. The four solos indicated the direction the band was headed.

The End

In September 1969, around the same time *Abbey Road* was released, John told the other Beatles that he was leaving the band. He wanted to concentrate on making music with Yoko and working for peace. Although Paul, George, and Ringo also began working on solo projects, the Beatles did not officially announce that the band was breaking up for several months. Allen Klein was afraid the news would hurt sales of the album *Let It Be*, which was due to be released in the spring.

Paul finally broke the silence. He was very angry about the way *Let It Be* had turned out. Instead of being a simple rock album, Phil Spector had added orchestra music and backup singers to several songs. Paul insisted that the record be changed, but the other Beatles refused. On April 10, 1970, Paul announced that he was leaving the group because of "personal, business, and musical differences." John, George, and Ringo quickly confirmed the news that the Beatles would never perform together again.

After the breakup of the Beatles, all the group's former members had successful careers, something that doesn't always happen when a band splits. George, shown in this photo from 1975, released some albums and worked on behalf of charitable organizations. He also founded a record and film company. Sadly, he died from cancer in 2001.

5

Life After the Beatles

After the Beatles broke up, John, Paul, George, and Ringo each moved on to successful solo music careers. All four released hit singles and best-selling albums. However, each found that it was impossible to shake the label "Beatles." Throughout the 1970s, all four were constantly asked whether the band would ever reunite.

Both George and Ringo enjoyed their greatest successes during the early 1970s. George's 1970 album *All Things Must Pass* sold over 6 million copies and included several hit singles. The next year, George held a concert to raise money for the people of Bangladesh, a South Asian country that had just broken away from Pakistan. However, George's later albums never matched the popularity of *All Things Must Pass*, and he gradually withdrew from the music scene. To keep busy, he established a record company, Dark Horse Records, and a movie production company called Handmade Films.

In 1971 and 1973, Ringo released the top-5 singles "It Don't Come Easy" and "Back Off Boogaloo." He followed up with the 1973 album *Ringo*, which sold more than a million copies and produced a pair of #1 hits, "Photograph" and "You're Sixteen." John, Paul, and George each played with Ringo on the album, although not together. Like George, Ringo also gradually withdrew from music to pursue an acting career, with roles in such films as *Son of Dracula* (1974) and *Caveman* (1981). Later, he played the narrator on the British children's television program *Thomas the Tank Engine and Friends*.

Success and Tragedy

Paul's post-Beatles career was extremely productive. In 1971, he formed a new band, Wings, which also included his wife Linda. During the 1970s, Wings had several major hits, including "Band on the Run," "Jet," and "Silly Love Songs." In the 1980s, Paul released several solo albums and also recorded duets with Stevie Wonder ("Ebony and Ivory") and Michael Jackson ("The Girl Is Mine," "Say Say Say"). These hits ensured his place as one of the top recording artists of the 1980s. Today, the *Guinness Book of World Records* lists Paul as the most successful musician and composer in history.

For several years there was a deep division between Paul and John. Once the closest of friends, shortly after the breakup, each released songs that insulted the other. But things changed in the mid-1970s, and gradually the two men resumed their friendship. They would never be as close as they had once been, but they enjoyed spending an occasional evening together in John's New York apartment talking about the good old days.

John continued his political activism along with his recording career. In his 1971 hit "Imagine," he sang about his hope that one day all people could live together peacefully. He and Yoko recorded several albums together in the early 1970s. When Yoko gave birth to their son Sean in October 1975, John decided to retire from music to care for the boy. But after five years away from the music business, he felt refreshed creatively and decided to make a new record with Yoko. Many of the songs on *Double Fantasy* (1980), such as "(Just Like) Starting Over," "Woman," "Watching the Wheels," and "Beautiful Boy" reflect the satisfaction John had finally found in his personal life.

WHY ANDY KAUFMAN IS NOT FUNNY ■ STEVE WINWOOD
GARY U.S. BONDS ■ LOUIS MALLE ON AMERICAN SLEAZE

NO. 342 APRIL 30TH, 1981
$1.50 UK 60P

RollingStone

Taking
RINGO
Seriously
[Mr. Starkey at 40]

Ringo's post-Beatle career included an appearance on
the cover of *Rolling Stone* in 1981. He had hit albums and
singles, but he moved away from music and became an
actor. Children all over the world recognize the former
Beatle as the narrator on the British children's show
Thomas the Tank Engine and Friends.

Paul found almost instant success as a former Beatle with his new group, Wings. Formed in 1971, the band included his wife, Linda, shown fourth from left in this photo from 1976. Paul also released solo albums and duets. In recognition of his contributions to music, Paul was knighted by Queen Elizabeth II in 1976.

Tragically, John did not live to see the album's success. While walking to his New York apartment on the evening of December 8, 1980, he was shot and killed by a deranged fan named Mark David Chapman. People all over the world mourned. Yoko eventually paid for a memorial park, called Strawberry Fields, to be constructed in New York's Central Park, near the place where John was shot. Each year thousands of people visit Strawberry Fields on December 8 to sing John's songs and remember him.

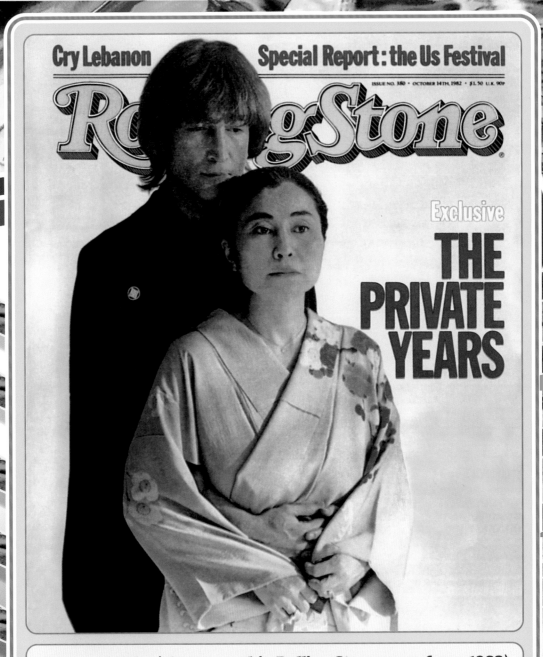

Cry Lebanon   Special Report: the Us Festival

Rolling Stone

ISSUE NO. 380 • OCTOBER 14TH, 1982 • $1.50 U.K. 90P

Exclusive

THE PRIVATE YEARS

John and Yoko (shown on this *Rolling Stone* cover from 1982) married, continued to be political activists, and even recorded together. But John's biggest success post-Beatles was as a solo artist, with such major hits as "Imagine." When their son Sean was born, John became a full-time father. The rock legend was murdered in 1980 by a fan.

Coming Together Again

The murder of John Lennon ended the dream of many fans that the Beatles would get back together one day. Legal battles over control of Apple Corps, which stretched into the early 1990s, prolonged the bitter feelings among the surviving Beatles. When the Beatles were inducted into the Rock and Roll Hall of Fame in 1988, Paul decided not to attend the ceremony because of the unresolved issues. George and Ringo did attend the ceremony, however, and Yoko joined them to represent John.

Once the legal issues surrounding Apple Corps were resolved, Paul agreed to collaborate with the other surviving Beatles and Yoko on a documentary about the group. Everyone who had been involved with the band, including George Martin and Neil Aspinall (who had been the band's road manager during the 1960s), gave extensive interviews. Old recordings and movies from the Apple Corps archives were dusted off and reviewed.

Over two nights in the fall of 1995, the U.S. television network ABC broadcast the six-hour documentary *The Beatles Anthology*. In addition to the interviews, which gave an amazing inside view of the Beatles' lives during the 1960s, the documentary also included many never-before-seen photos and film clips. The program was one of the highest-rated shows of the year, and received a Grammy Award in 1996.

Beatles Songs Old and New

While working on the *Anthology* project, the Beatles combed through hundreds of hours of their old recordings. The tapes included many **outtakes**, alternate versions of songs, and even some songs that had been finished but never released. The best of this material was included on three double albums, which were released separately in 1995 and 1996. Beatles fans who listened to the tracks felt they provided new insights into the way the four Beatles had worked with George Martin to create their distinctive sound in the recording studio.

In addition to the old material, the three surviving Beatles returned to the studio to produce two new songs for the *Anthology* albums. Yoko had provided tapes of John singing several unfinished songs, and the other Beatles recorded lyrics and music to accompany him. The first song, "Free as a Bird," was first heard at the end of the documentary broadcast. It reached #6 on the *Billboard* chart in the United States and won a pair of Grammy Awards in 1996, for Best Music Video Short Form and Best Pop Performance by a Duo or Group with Vocal. The second new song, "Real Love," was released a few months later with the second *Anthology* album. It hit #11 on the U.S. *Billboard* chart.

Paul later mentioned how much he had enjoyed making the new songs:

> **"So we had these two tracks that had been a really great pleasure to work on. . . . It really was just the Beatles. The great thing was we were locked with the demo. You couldn't change it much so the style was set by John. It was a laugh, we had a great laugh."**

Other Releases

In addition to the *Anthology* albums, Beatles fans could find other new recordings of the band during the 1990s and early 2000s. In 1994, Apple Corps released a two-CD collection of rare Beatles recordings made for the BBC between 1962 and 1965. *The Beatles Live at the BBC* included unreleased live versions of nine of the band's own songs, including "I Saw Her Standing There," "I'm A Loser," and "Thank You Girl." However, most of the fifty-six tracks were cover versions of songs by some of the group's favorite artists, including Buddy Holly, Carl Perkins, Chuck Berry, Ray Charles, and Elvis Presley.

In 1999, a remastered version of the soundtrack to *Yellow Submarine* was released. The next year, Apple followed up with a compilation album containing every Beatles song to hit number one in the United States or United Kingdom. Titled simply *1*, this album sold more than 12 million copies in its first three weeks of release, making it the fastest-selling album of all time. By 2007, *1* had sold more than 30 million copies worldwide.

In 2003, the album *Let It Be . . . Naked* was released. It included most of the songs from the original *Let It Be* album, but without the orchestration and background singers that Phil Spector had added. The album cover is very similar to the original cover for *Let It Be*,

LET IT BE

Fans still love the Beatles, and sales of the group's remastered and re-released albums show that love and respect. In 2003, *Let It Be . . . Naked* was released. Missing from the re-release were the things that made the group dislike the original—heavy orchestration and background singers. The original cover (shown here), was altered somewhat.

although the images appear in negative. The only image that changed was George Harrison's—a smiling picture was used on the original cover, while an alternate shot of him looking downcast was used on the new version. This was done intentionally, because George had died from cancer in November 2001.

Love Is All You Need

It was in 2003 that Apple Corps gave approval for Cirque du Soleil to proceed with the *Love* show. George Martin and his son Giles were hired to create a soundtrack for the show from the Beatles' original recordings. When the show premiered in 2006, it was obvious that they had succeeded. As reviewer Roger Friedman wrote after the opening:

> **"The show [has] a magical combination of acrobatics, ballet, video and fanciful sets and costumes. . . . *Love* is just an exhilarating, phenomenal show, one that will not only revive the Beatles catalog but bring their music to a whole new generation."**

The Beatles remain the standard by which all rock musicians must be judged. Although the band broke up more than thirty-five years ago, Beatles songs continue to be played on radio stations, and their records still have strong sales. Dozens of books about the band and its impact on popular culture are published each year. John, Paul, George, and Ringo continue to fascinate and appeal to a new generation of fans. Perhaps a comment made by George during the *Anthology* interviews best explains the reason for the band's long-standing appeal:

> **"I think we gave hope to the Beatle fans. We gave them a positive feeling that there was a sunny day ahead and that there was a good time to be had. . . . There were those kinds of messages in a lot of our songs."**

1940 Richard Starkey (better known as Ringo Starr) is born on July 7; John Lennon is born on October 9.

1942 Paul McCartney is born on June 18.

1943 George Harrison is born on February 25.

1957 In March, John Lennon starts a skiffle band called the Quarry Men; John meets Paul, and invites him to join the group.

1958 George Harrison is invited to join the Quarry Men.

1960 The Quarry Men tour northern Scotland as a backup band for singer Johnny Gentle; in May the group is renamed the Silver Beatles, later changed to the Beatles; Pete Best joins the band as drummer in August, and the Beatles begin performing at nightclubs in Hamburg, Germany.

1961 The Beatles are asked to serve as the backup band for singer Tony Sheridan; Brian Epstein hears the band and offers to become their manager.

1962 George Martin of EMI agrees to work with the Beatles, and helps them produce several singles.

1963 "Please Please Me" hits #1;; the Beatles make their first album, *Please Please Me*.

1964 Beatlemania sweeps across the United States after the Beatles appear on the *Ed Sullivan Show* in February. In April, the band's singles hold the top five spots on the Billboard music chart; John's first book, *In His Own Write*, is published and quickly becomes a bestseller; the film *A Hard Day's Night* becomes an international success, as does the soundtrack album; In December, the album *Beatles for Sale* is released.

1965 The Beatles release their second film, *Help!*; on August 15 the Beatles play a landmark concert at Shea Stadium in New York before 55,000 fans; in October, John, Paul, George, and Ringo receive medals from the Queen.

1966 The Beatles decide to stop touring after problems in the Philippines and the United States.

1967 *Sgt Pepper's Lonely Hearts Club Band* is released to critical and popular acclaim; the Beatles perform "All You Need Is Love" on the world's first satellite broadcast; Brian Epstein dies on August 27; Apple Corps is formed to oversee the Beatles' business interests; in December the Beatles release *Magical Mystery Tour*, which receives poor reviews.

1968 The Beatles study transcendental meditation in India with the Maharishi Mahesh Yogi; John begins dating Yoko Ono; the animated film *Yellow Submarine* is released in July; the double album *The Beatles* (better known as the "White Album") is released in November.

1969 The Beatles begin filming and recording music for the Get Back project; John tells the other Beatles that he is leaving the group, although this is kept secret.

1970 Paul McCartney's first solo album is released in April, and he announces that the Beatles have broken up; in May, the album *Let It Be* is released; in December Paul files a lawsuit to dissolve the Beatles' partnership.

1980 Mark David Chapman murders John Lennon on December 8.

1988 The Beatles are inducted into the Rock and Roll Hall of Fame.

1994 The two-disc album *The Beatles Live at the BBC* is released.

1995 *The Beatles Anthology*, a documentary, is aired on ABC television.

1996 The albums *Anthology II* and *Anthology III* are released.

1999 Apple Corps issues a remastered soundtrack to the film *Yellow Submarine*.

2000 A compilation of the Beatles' #1 hits, titled *1*, becomes the fastest-selling album of all time.

2001 George Harrison dies of cancer on November 29.

2003 The album *Let It Be . . . Naked* is released to mixed reviews.

2006 The show *Love* opens in Las Vegas to rave reviews; in November, the soundtrack to the show is released and quickly sells a million copies.

Albums

1963 *Please Please Me*
With the Beatles

1964 *A Hard Day's Night*
Beatles for Sale

1965 *Help!*
Rubber Soul

1966 *Revolver*

1967 *Sgt Pepper's Lonely Hearts Club Band*
Magical Mystery Tour

1968 *Yellow Submarine*
The Beatles (the "White Album,")

1969 *Abbey Road*

1970 *Let It Be*

Number-One Singles

1964 "I Want to Hold Your Hand"
"She Loves You"
"Can't Buy Me Love"
"Love Me Do"
"A Hard Day's Night"
"I Feel Fine"

1965 "Eight Days a Week"
"Ticket to Ride"
"Help!"
"Yesterday"
"We Can Work It Out"

1966 "Paperback Writer"

1967 "Penny Lane"
"All You Need Is Love"
"Hello, Goodbye"

1968 "Hey Jude"

1969 "Get Back"
"Come Together"/"Something"

1970 "Let It Be"
"The Long and Winding Road"

Movies

1964 *A Hard Day's Night*

1965 *Help!*

1968 *Yellow Submarine*
1970 *Let It Be*

Television
1967 *Magical Mystery Tour*

Select Awards

1964 Grammy Awards: Best New Artist, Best Performance by a Vocal Group (*A Hard Day's Night*).

1966 Grammy Awards: Best Contemporary Pop Vocal Performance, Male (Paul McCartney for "Eleanor Rigby"), Best Album Cover/Package (*Revolver*), Song of the Year ("Michelle").

1967 Grammy Awards: Album of the Year, Best Contemporary Album, Best Album Cover, Best Engineered (Non-Classical) Recording (all for *Sgt. Pepper's Lonely Hearts Club Band*).

1970 Grammy Award: Best Original Score Written for a Motion Picture of TV Special ("Let It Be"); Academy Awards: Best Original Song Score ("Let It Be").

1972 National Academy of Recording Arts and Sciences: Trustee Award.

1975 Grammy Hall of Fame Induction (as a group).

1993 Grammy Hall of Fame Induction (*Sgt. Pepper's Lonely Hearts Club Band*).

1995 Grammy Hall of Fame Induction (*Abbey Road*).

1996 Grammy Award: Best Pop Performance by a Duo or Group with Vocal, Best Music Video Short Form (both for "Free as a Bird), Best Music Video Long Form (*The Beatles Anthology*).

1997 Grammy Hall of Fame Induction ("Yesterday").

1998 Grammy Hall of Fame Induction ("I Want to Hold Your Hand").

1999 Grammy Hall of Fame Induction (*Revolver*).

2000 Grammy Hall of Fame Induction (*Rubber Soul*, *A Hard Day's Night*, *The Beatles*).

2001 Grammy Hall of Fame Induction ("Hey Jude," *Meet the Beatles*).

2002 Grammy Hall of Fame Induction ("Eleanor Rigby").

2004 Grammy Hall of Fame Induction ("Let It Be"); National Academy of Recording Arts and Sciences: Presidents' Award.

Books

The Beatles. *The Beatles Anthology*. San Francisco, Calif.: Chronicle Books, 2000.

Hill, Tim, and Marie Clayton, eds. *The Beatles Unseen Archives*. Bath, U.K.: Parragon Publishing, 2004.

Lennon, John, and Jann S. Wenner. *Lennon Remembers*. New York: W. W. Norton, 2001.

Miles, Barry. *Paul McCartney: Many Years from Now*. New York: Henry Holt, 1998.

Spitz, Bob. *The Beatles: The Biography*. Boston: Little, Brown and Company, 2005.

Stark, Steven D. *Meet the Beatles: A Cultural History of the Band that Shook Youth, Gender, and the World*. New York: Harper Entertainment, 2005.

Web Sites

www.beatles.com
The Beatles Official Web Site

www.cirquedusoleil.com/CirqueDuSoleil/en/showstickets/love/ intro/intro.htm
Love Official Web Site

www.georgeharrison.com
George Harrison Official Web Site

www.johnlennon.com
John Lennon Official Web Site

www.paulmccartney.com/main.php
Paul McCartney Official Web Site

www.ringostarr.com
Ringo Starr Official Web Site

www.rockhall.com/hof/inductee.asp?id=228
Rock and Roll Hall of Fame, Beatles Induction Page

www.time.com/time/time100/artists/profile/beatles.html
The *Time* 100 Beatles page

audacious—Bold, daring, or fearless.

avant-garde—Artwork or music that is new or experimental and is significantly different from the norm.

demo tape—A collection of songs intended to show off the skills of a performer to a record producer.

double album—A long album that requires two complete records or CDs to contain all of the music.

double-tracked—Recorded in a way that allowed the performer to sing along with a prerecorded track to create a richer, stronger sound.

guru—A religious teacher or spiritual guide.

innovators—People who change the way things are done or who do things in a new way.

mash-up—A musical genre in which two or more different songs are combined to create a new musical track.

montage—A creation of something from many small pieces.

outtakes—Recordings that do not appear on the final version of an album, usually because they contain mistakes.

psychedelic—Imitating, suggestive of, or reproducing effects associated with certain types of drugs, such as LSD.

skiffle—A type of music played using nontraditional instruments, such as washboards, jugs, or tea-chest basses, in addition to guitars and banjos.

soundtrack—Music from a film, video, or television show.

venues—Locations for performances.

yoga—A Hindu philosophical school that focuses on meditation as the path to self-knowledge.

Jim Gallagher is the author of more than two dozen books for young adults. He lives in Stockton, New Jersey, with his wife, LaNelle, and their two sons, Dillon and Donald.

Picture Credits